The Rocky Road

BY
WILLIAM B DRUMMOND

THE ROCKY ROAD
The True Story of Sylvester Stallone's Path to Fame

The Rocky Road

The True Story of Sylvester Stallone's Path to Fame.

By

William B. Drummond

The Rocky Road

All rights reserved. No part of this publication may be reproduced, distributed, or transmitted in any form or by any means, including photocopying, recording, or other electronic or mechanical methods, without the prior written permission of the publisher, except in the case of brief quotations embodied in critical reviews and certain other noncommercial uses permitted by copyright law.

Copyright © William B. Drummond, 2023.

The Rocky Road

TABLE OF CONTENTS

Introduction

Chapter 1

Chapter 2

Chapter 3

Chapter 4

Chapter 5

Introduction

Welcome to "The Rocky Road: The True Story of Sylvester Stallone's Path to Fame", a book that digs deep into the extraordinary journey of one of Hollywood's most legendary performers.

Sylvester Stallone is a name that resonates with followers throughout the world. He has captivated us with his great performances in classic blockbusters like Rocky, Rambo, and The Expendables. Yet below the flash and splendor comes a narrative of suffering, tenacity, and endurance.

"The Rocky Road" takes you on a rollercoaster trip through the highs and lows of Stallone's life. From his modest origins in New York City to his ascent to prominence, you'll get an intimate glimpse at the man behind the movies. You'll uncover the hurdles Stallone experienced when attempting to enter the film business. You'll discover his tireless pursuit of his ambitions, his determination to give up, and the sacrifices he took to attain success. You'll be inspired by his persistence, determination, and his ability to overcome extraordinary difficulties. This book isn't simply about Sylvester Stallone's ascent to stardom; it's also a narrative of the human spirit. It's about the power of self-belief, hard effort, and dedication. It's about how, no matter how hard our aspirations may appear, with the correct mentality and attitude, we can accomplish anything.

"The Rocky Road" is a must-read for everyone who likes movies, is interested in the entertainment business or is seeking inspiration in their path. This book is a monument to Stallone's incredible life and a reminder that everything is possible if we believe in ourselves and stay the course. So, sit back, relax, and get ready for a voyage through the life of one of Hollywood's greatest performers. This is "The Rocky Road: The Real Story of Sylvester Stallone's Journey to Fame".

Chapter 1
Born to Be a Fighter: Stallone's Early Years in New York City

Sylvester Stallone was born on July 6, 1946, in New York City. He was the oldest son of Frank Stallone Sr. and Jacqueline "Jackie" Stallone. From an early age, Stallone was attracted to the arts, especially acting. He spent most of his youth watching movies, reading books, and dreaming of one day being an actor. Yet, Stallone's early years were not without their problems. His family was not well-off, and they battled to make ends meet. Stallone's parents also had a turbulent relationship, which regularly ended in disputes and fights. Notwithstanding these hurdles, Stallone remained determined to achieve his objectives. He attended the American College of Switzerland in Leysin, where he studied acting and got active in theatrical plays. After returning to the United States, Stallone enrolled at the University of Miami, where he continued to pursue acting.

In the early 1970s, Stallone went to New York City, where he took odd jobs to make ends meet. He frequently slept around bus stops and struggled to find stable employment as an actor. Notwithstanding these dissatisfactions, Stallone continued to write and appear in plays, polishing his art and expanding his abilities. It was at this period that Stallone developed the story for what would become his blockbuster picture, "Rocky". The plot was inspired by Stallone's difficulties

The Rocky Road

and experiences, and he put his heart and soul into the writing. Unfortunately, it was not an easy route to having the film created. Stallone endured numerous rejections and setbacks and even turned down a huge amount of money for the rights to the screenplay when he was informed he could not feature in the picture. Yet Stallone's patience paid off. Finally, he was able to persuade executives to let him feature in the picture, and "Rocky" became a major blockbuster, making over $225 million worldwide and winning three Oscar Awards, including Best Picture.

Stallone's early years in New York City were distinguished by adversity, effort, and dedication. After experiencing several challenges and disappointments, he refused to give up on his ambitions. His experiences during this period helped define the actor and writer he would become and gave the idea for one of the most cherished films of all time. Stallone's experiences in New York City have affected his personal and professional outlook. He learned to work hard and endure in the face of hardship, which became a distinguishing trait of his career. Stallone also acquired a strong feeling of commitment to his family and friends, which would inspire many of his cinematic endeavors.

In addition to his career as a writer and actor, Stallone also got active in bodybuilding and fitness during his early years in New York City. He trained at the legendary Gold's Gym and participated in various bodybuilding contests. His devotion to fitness and physical power would become a trademark of his career, as he routinely did his stunts and took on physically demanding jobs. Stallone's early experiences also featured some key partnerships. He married his first wife, Sasha Czack, in 1974, and the pair had two children together. They divorced in 1985. He also forged a strong acquaintance with fellow actor and action icon Arnold Schwarzenegger during this period, with the two regularly exercising together and discussing their professional objectives.

The Rocky Road

Nevertheless, Stallone's early years in New York City were a crucial moment for the actor and writer. His trials and triumphs during this period would help influence his professional and personal beliefs for years to come. Although confronting several hurdles and disappointments, Stallone's perseverance and passion for his profession helped him to achieve immense success and become one of the most revered and legendary people in Hollywood history.

An Uphill Battle: Stallone's Effort to Get Into the Film Industry

After years of hard work and effort, Sylvester Stallone finally found success with his breakthrough movie, "Rocky". The picture was a critical and economic triumph and propelled Stallone to prominence nearly overnight. But, Stallone's road to the top was far from simple. In truth, he had toiled for years to break into the film business and gain the respect he deserved. Stallone's early efforts to get into the film

The Rocky Road

business were greeted with frustration and failure. He constantly struggled to obtain employment as an actor and was often informed that he didn't have the necessary appearance or skill for the job. He also endured rejection as a writer, with several of his projects being rejected by studios and producers. Despite these disappointments, he refused to give up on his ambitions. He continued to perfect his trade and work on his acting talents and also penned many scripts in his leisure time. One of these scripts was "Rocky", which he had initially written as a vehicle for himself to act in.

But, when Stallone originally proposed the concept to producers, he experienced pushback. Many people were afraid to invest in a film with an unknown actor and offered Stallone significant amounts of money for the rights to the screenplay on the condition that he did not feature in the film. Stallone declined, arguing that he was the only one who could bring the role of Rocky Balboa to life.

After years of striving and rejection, Stallone eventually found a producer that believed in him and the idea for "Rocky". *Irwin Winkler* and *Robert Chartoff* took a gamble on the film and decided to let Stallone feature in the starring role. The rest, as they say, is history. "Rocky" became one of the most popular pictures of all time, making over **$225 million** worldwide and winning three Academy Awards.

Unfortunately, Stallone's problems in the film business did not stop with "Rocky". Despite the popularity of the film, he continued to experience criticism from producers and reviewers who denied his skill and aptitude as an actor. He was typically typecast in action roles and struggled to break out of this pattern and take on more diversified parts. Stallone also suffered personal challenges at this time, including a tough divorce from his first wife, Sasha Czack, and a period of addiction to drugs and alcohol. Yet, he stayed motivated to overcome these hurdles and continue his career in the film business.

Throughout the years, Stallone has continued to work hard to accomplish success in the film industry. He has appeared in multiple blockbuster films, including the "Rocky" trilogy, "Rambo", and "The Expendables". He has also gained critical recognition for his work as an actor and director, garnering multiple prizes and nominations.

Stallone's route to success in the film business was an uphill fight, fraught with rejection and disappointments. Nonetheless, his tenacity and endurance helped him to overcome these difficulties and fulfill his ambitions. His narrative is a tribute to the power of hard work and determination and serves as an example to aspiring performers and filmmakers throughout the globe.

In conclusion, the uphill fight Stallone fought to get into the film business is a testimonial of his everlasting devotion to his work. Despite countless disappointments and hurdles, he refused to give up on his aspirations and worked relentlessly to attain success as an actor, writer, and director. His narrative serves as an example to anybody who has encountered rejection or struggled with their ambitions, and his influence in the film business will continue to be felt for centuries to come.

The Creation of Rocky: How Stallone Defied the Odds to Build a Classic Standard Movie

"The Creation of Rocky" is a tale of one man's drive to make his goal a reality, despite insurmountable obstacles and endless disappointments. The guy was Sylvester Stallone, and the dream was a film about an underdog fighter called Rocky Balboa. Stallone created the screenplay for "Rocky" in only three days, taking inspiration from his own experiences as an aspiring actor and boxer. Yet, getting the film created proved to be a huge wrangle. Stallone was unknown in Hollywood at this time, and the screenplay was rejected by multiple studios before being picked up by United Artists.

The Rocky Road

Even after getting financed, Stallone encountered several hurdles throughout the shooting process. The budget was exceedingly low, and the team had to be inventive to make the most of their limited resources. Much of the film's most memorable moments, like the training montage and the final battle, were filmed in only a few takes. Stallone also received mistrust from several members of the cast and crew, who challenged his ability to carry the picture as both the writer and actor. Nonetheless, Stallone's zeal and devotion to the project proved contagious, and he won over even his most hesitant partners.

Despite the hurdles, "Rocky" was a critical and economic triumph, generating over $225 million worldwide and winning three Academy Awards, including Best Picture. The film's influence has persisted for nearly four decades, influencing other filmmakers and establishing Stallone's status as one of Hollywood's most legendary personalities.

The Rocky Road

The narrative of "The Creation of Rocky" is a monument to Stallone's unshakable perseverance and artistic vision. Against all odds, he fought the critics and brought his ambition to life on the big screen, producing a timeless masterpiece that continues to connect with viewers to this day. The film's ongoing success is a monument to the power of narrative, and the influence that one person's vision can have on the world.

One of the primary things that made "Rocky" such a hit was the way it tapped into the cultural zeitgeist of the period. The film was released in 1976, at a period when many Americans were feeling disillusioned and alienated. The Vietnam War had just finished, and the Watergate affair had shattered the public's faith in their government. In this background, "Rocky" struck a chord with viewers by giving a tale of optimism and resilience in the face of apparently insurmountable difficulties. The character of Rocky Balboa symbolized the American spirit of persistence and drive, and his effort to overcome adversity resonated with viewers throughout the country.

The film's popularity also had a tremendous influence on Stallone's career. Before "Rocky", he had been trying to obtain employment as an actor and had even pondered giving up on his ambition of making it in Hollywood. Yet, the film's popularity drove him to superstardom, and he went on to become one of the greatest cinema stars of the 1980s and 90s.

In addition to starting Stallone's career, "Rocky" also had a lasting influence on the cinema industry as a whole. The film's underdog tale and gritty, realistic approach inspired a wave of similarly themed films in the years that followed, including "Raging Bull" and "The Fighter".

Nowadays, "Rocky" is largely recognized as one of the greatest sports films of all time, and its effect on popular culture can still be felt almost four decades after its premiere. The narrative of its production serves as a poignant reminder of the value of tenacity and creative vision in the face of hardship, and its lasting appeal is a monument to the power of great storytelling.

Chapter 2

Fame and Fortune: Stallone's Climb to Superstardom in Hollywood.

With the triumph of "Rocky", Sylvester Stallone became one of Hollywood's most sought-after actors. He followed up the picture with a streak of successes, including "First Blood", "Rambo: First Blood Part II", and "Rocky III". These films reinforced his image as a huge box-office attraction, and he quickly became one of the highest-paid performers in Hollywood.

Stallone's ascension to superstardom was a mix of skill, hard work, and astute commercial acumen. He was not happy to rest on his laurels following the success of "Rocky", and instead he set his eyes on forging a long-lasting career in the film business. He deliberately picked jobs that would highlight his variety as an actor and appeal to a broad audience and was prepared to take risks in pursuit of his ambitions.

One of the secrets to Stallone's success was his ability to connect with people on a human level. He had a rough, manly attitude that appealed to both men and women, and his characters generally reflected the ideals of hard labor, tenacity, and devotion. He was also not hesitant to tackle tough and contentious issues in his films, such as the Vietnam War and the treatment of prisoners of war.

The Rocky Road

Stallone's success also owes much to his financial savvy. He was a smart negotiator and was able to win rich arrangements for his films and items. He also took charge of his career by writing and directing several of his films and was ready to take creative risks in pursuit of his vision. Yet, Stallone's triumph was not without its hurdles. He attracted criticism from certain places for his tough-guy demeanor and was accused of propagating bad notions of masculinity. He also faced competition from other growing stars in the business, such as Arnold Schwarzenegger and Bruce Willis.

Notwithstanding these hurdles, Stallone managed to prosper in Hollywood during the 1980s and 90s. He starred in multiple popular films, including "Cliffhanger", "Demolition Man", and "The Expendables" trilogy. He also continued to experiment and take chances in his profession, such as his stint as a supporting player in "Cop Land", which displayed his versatility as an actor.

The Rocky Road

Currently, Stallone is largely considered one of Hollywood's most legendary individuals. His effect on popular culture can still be felt today, as his films continue to inspire and excite audiences across the globe. The narrative of his ascent to superstardom is a monument to the power of talent, hard effort, and creative vision in the film business, and a reminder that success is always within reach for those ready to take it.

The Rocky Road

Rocky II, III, and Beyond: Stallone's Continuing Success in Film.

One of the most recognizable and adored movie franchises of all time is the Rocky series starring Sylvester Stallone. For more than 40 years, audiences all around the globe have been inspired by the tale of a Philadelphia boxer who began as an underdog and eventually rose to become a champion. Rocky Balboa's journey through the world of professional boxing was followed by multiple sequels after the 1976 success of the original Rocky movie, which was directed by Sylvester Stallone. This article will discuss the Rocky II, III, and Beyond movies and how Stallone's depiction of Rocky had a significant role in the actor's continued success in the movie business.

Rock II (1979)

Rocky II takes up where the previous movie left off, with Rocky having fallen to Apollo Creed in their title match. Rocky's struggles to reconstruct his life and reclaim his confidence both inside and outside of the ring are followed throughout the movie. Along the way, he marries Talia Shire's character Adrian, and starts getting ready for a rematch with Creed.

With over $200 million in box office revenue, Rocky II was both a critical and financial triumph. It received plaudits for how well it portrayed Rocky and for Stallone's dual roles as the movie's writer and actor. Rocky became one of the most recognizable characters in movie history as a result of the movie's themes of tenacity, willpower, and the strength of love and family, which connected with viewers all over the globe.

Rocky III (1982)
Rocky III was a change from the first two movies in that it placed more of an emphasis on the glitter and glamor of the professional boxing scene. In the movie, Rocky competes against Clubber Lang, portrayed by Mr. T, who is a more fearsome and ferocious foe than any opponent Rocky has ever faced. Rocky is forced to face his concerns and doubts along the road, while Apollo Creed, a new mentor, offers him

advice and instruction. With over $270 million in box office receipts, Rocky III was yet another box office hit. It received accolades for its intense combat sequences, examination of the shadowy side of celebrity and success, and chemistry between Stallone and his co-stars, Mr. T and Carl Weathers as Apollo Creed. The popular song "Eye of the Tiger" by Survivor was included on the soundtrack, which also went on to become a cultural phenomenon and is still well-known today.

Rocky Above (1990-)
Rocky IV (1985), Rocky V (1990), Rocky Balboa (2006), Creed (2015), and Creed II are just a few of the several sequels that Stallone produced for the Rocky series (2018). Each movie focused on a different aspect of Rocky, such as his connection with his son, his decision to give up boxing, or his role as a mentor to a new generation of fighters.

As it is often referred to, Rocky Beyond has remained a hit for Stallone and the movie business. It is impossible to overestimate the franchise's influence on popular culture, which has brought in over $1.7 billion globally. Rocky Balboa's persona has come to represent tenacity, grit, and the ability of the human spirit to triumph over even the most difficult challenges.

Sylvester Stallone's Rocky trilogy has grown to be one of the most adored and enduring movie series of all time, and his depiction of Rocky has been a significant contributor to his ongoing success in the movie business. Rocky Balboa has become a figure of hope and inspiration for many people because of the themes of endurance, dedication, the strength of love, and family that are important to the Rocky movies.

The Expendables: How Stallone Reinvigorated His Career in the 21st Century.

Sylvester Stallone's legendary performances in films like Rocky and Rambo helped him become one of Hollywood's greatest stars in the late

The Rocky Road

1970s and early 1980s. Yet once the 1990s arrived, Stallone's career began to sputter and he had trouble landing parts that connected with viewers. Stallone didn't rediscover his mojo until the twenty-first century, and that's all because of The Expendables. The Expendables, Stallone's passion project, was released in 2010. When they set out on a mission to oust a terrible tyrant, a crew of mercenaries played by an all-star ensemble of action movie veterans are followed in the film. Together with Jason Statham, Jet Li, Dolph Lundgren, Mickey Rourke, and others, Stallone wrote, directed, and starred in the film. The Expendables was an homage to the legendary action films of the 1980s and 1990s, and it rapidly won over viewers who missed that period. The film was a huge hit, earning over $274 million globally and inspiring two sequels. The Expendables had a significant influence on Stallone's career beyond its box-office triumph. It demonstrated that despite being close to 60, he still had what it takes to be a starring man in Hollywood. A new generation of fans who weren't old enough to recall Stallone's glory years in the 1980s was also reintroduced to him via the film. Stallone had fresh possibilities in Hollywood as a result of his performance in The Expendables. He went on to appear in critically acclaimed and financially successful films including Escape Plan, Creed, and Guardians of the Galaxy Vol. 2.

The Expendables' greatest influence, though, may have been in opening up opportunities for other action movie stars to make comebacks. The Last Stand, which featured Arnold Schwarzenegger, and Red, which starred Bruce Willis, were two examples of movies that were made in response to the popularity of The Expendables. The Expendables was a turning moment in Sylvester Stallone's career, to sum up. It demonstrated his continued viability as a leading man in Hollywood and reconnected him with his previous audience. The film's popularity also provided Stallone with fresh chances and made it possible for other action movie stars to return. The Expendables will be remembered as a timeless action film that revitalized Sylvester

Stallone's career and established a new genre for action films in the twenty-first century.

Off-screen relationships and family life of Sylvester Stallone

For more than 40 years, Sylvester Stallone has been a household figure in Hollywood. Although he is most known for his famous on-screen performances, there is also plenty to be said about his private life. Stallone has a large family and has been married many times during his career. This is a thorough look into Stallone's family and personal ties. Sasha Czack was Stallone's first wife, whom he wedded in 1974. Sage and Seargeoh, the couple's two boys, were born to them. Sage became an actor like his father before him, but Seargeoh, who is autistic, has generally avoided the spotlight.

But Stallone and Czack's marriage did not last, and they split up in 1985. Afterward, Stallone acknowledged that his career suffered as a consequence of his battle with depression at this time. Stallone wed Brigitte Nielsen, a model, and actress, as his second wife in 1985. After just two years, their brief marriage ended in divorce. Stallone wed model and businesswoman Jennifer Flavin in his third marriage. Since their marriage in 1997, they have remained together. Sophia, Sistine, and Scarlet are the three girls that the couple has together.

Stallone has made a point of emphasizing the value of his family and the part they play in his life. He said in a Men's Journal interview "I have so much to say about my family. They keep me in my place. They keep me in check."

Also, Stallone has been candid about the difficulties he has had as a dad. He discussed his son Seargeoh's autism and the challenges it presents in a conversation with The Guardian. He stated: "While in difficulties, you must persevere. To ensure that kids have happy lives, you must provide for them, cherish them, and do all in your power."

Stallone has throughout the years developed deep bonds with his co-stars in addition to his children. He was very close to Burgess Meredith, his co-star in the film Rocky, and was saddened by his death in 1997. Moreover, Stallone was good friends of Bruce Willis and Arnold Schwarzenegger, both of whom he collaborated with on The Expendables. Despite his ups and downs, Stallone continues to be one of Hollywood's most recognizable and adored actors. He is a loving father who has remained connected to his family and friends throughout his professional life. Even the largest Hollywood stars have families, friends, and personal issues outside of the limelight, as Stallone's personal life serves as a reminder. Stallone routinely publishes pictures and videos of himself with his wife and children on social media, which demonstrates his love and commitment to his family. He often uses sincere captions to say how much they mean to him and how appreciative he is of their love and support.

The bond between Stallone and his kids has also come up for criticism over time. Several people have speculated about his bond with his late son Sage in particular. Sage, unfortunately, died away in 2012 at the age of 36, and it is obvious that Stallone was deeply affected by his passing.

He discussed the suffering of losing a kid in an interview with The Hollywood Reporter. He stated: "Losing a kid is an awful scenario. It's the worst experience a parent could have." "You have to enjoy the time you have together because you never know when it's going to be gone," he said while discussing the value of cherishing the time you spend with your loved ones. Yet, the scandal has dogged Stallone's personal life. He was charged in 2016 with sexually abusing a 16-year-old girl back in 1986. The accusations were strongly refuted by Stallone, and no charges were ever brought. Stallone's lawyer referred to the accusations as "totally false" in a statement.

Stallone has maintained his popularity in Hollywood despite this incident, and both fans and the media are still interested in learning about his personal life. Stallone has stayed committed to his family and his work throughout it all, and he has no intention of slowing down any time soon.

Chapter 3
The Art of Acting: Stallone's Approach to His Craft

Popular actor, author, and director Sylvester Stallone has made a lasting impression on the world of film with his renowned roles as John Rambo and Rocky Balboa. During his more than five-decade acting career, Stallone has created a

The Rocky Road

distinctive method for approaching the "art of acting," as he calls it. Stallone's method of acting is greatly affected by his life events and the difficulties he had in his early acting career. He has often discussed his efforts to get into the business and how he had to put in a lot of effort to establish his value as an actor. He thinks that acting is more than simply memorizing lines and delivering them well; it's also about comprehending the motives of the characters and bringing their emotions to life on film.

Stallone places a strong focus on physicality in his acting, which is one of his distinctive traits. He is renowned for his rigorous exercise regimens and the physical changes he makes in his roles. He thinks that a character's body is equally as substantial as their emotional complexity. An actor should be able to portray the emotions of the character via their body language and actions, according to Stallone.

The Rocky Road

Moreover, planning is really important to Stallone. He thinks that an actor needs to be completely ready before entering the set. This entails comprehending the character's past, goals, and connections to other characters. Stallone often spends weeks or even months getting ready for a part, entering the world of the character, and getting to know them on a deeply psychological level.

Stallone emphasizes the value of spontaneity in addition to athleticism and preparedness. A great actor, in his opinion, should be able to improvise when required and give the role their unique spin. Because of his talent for improvisation, Stallone often imbues the roles he plays with his style. Stallone's experiences as a writer and director have had a significant impact on his acting style. He feels that having written and directed multiple movies, notably the Rocky and Rambo series, has given him a special viewpoint on performing. He appreciates the value of good storytelling and how each character contributes to the overall plot. He also understands how to interact with actors and help them bring their roles to life on the screen.

Stallone has a comprehensive approach to acting in general. He thinks that acting is about inhabiting the characters and bringing their emotions to life, not merely memorizing lines and hitting their marks. In addition to emphasizing the value of physicality, preparation, improvisation, and narrative, he also believes that an actor should be completely dedicated to their trade. Stallone has solidified his position as one of the best performers of all time because of his extensive expertise in the field and distinctive style of acting.

Stallone's Struggle with Drug Addiction and Other Challenges: Overcoming Adversity.

One of today's most well-known and skilled actors is **Sylvester Stallone**. Stallone's career has spanned many decades and cemented his status as a household figure because of his memorable performances in films like Rocky and Rambo. Nonetheless, despite his celebrity and success, Stallone has had several hardships in his life, including a fight with addiction and other issues.

Stallone's battles with addiction started when he initially relocated to Hollywood to pursue his acting ambitions early in his career. He was a struggling actor at this time, trying to make ends meet, and he often used drink and drugs to deal with the stress and worry of his everyday existence.

Stallone was able to succeed in Hollywood despite his early difficulties with addiction. During the 1970s, he was cast in a series of tiny parts in films and TV programs, but it wasn't until 1976's Rocky that he got his big break. The movie was a huge hit, bringing Stallone critical praise and almost overnight making him a household figure.

Nonetheless, despite his newfound popularity, Stallone's battle with addiction persisted. His addiction started to negatively impact his personal and professional life as he persisted in abusing drugs and alcohol. His friendships and family were strained, and his work on the sets of movies got more irregular and unpredictable. At some time in the early 1980s, Stallone finally snapped. He came to see that his addiction was hurting not just his work but also his health, and relationships. He understood that if he wanted to continue working in Hollywood and leading a full life, he had to get sober and clean.

He entered a facility for treatment and started the arduous journey of healing. He learned new coping mechanisms to cope with stress and anxiety while working with addiction experts to address the root causes of his addiction. Also, he made an effort to restore his bonds with friends and family, offering sincere condolences and doing all in his power to make things right.

Stallone persisted despite the challenges of rehabilitation and was finally successful in beating his addiction. He has been sober for more than three decades and attributes his success in both his professional and personal lives to his recovery.

One of the numerous difficulties Stallone has experienced throughout his life is his fight with addiction. He has also had hardships with his health, his finances, and his personal life, but he has always managed to go through these obstacles and come out stronger on the other side. Stallone is now a beloved husband and father in addition to being a renowned actor. His films continue to enthrall audiences all around the globe, and he continues to work in Hollywood. Everyone who is fighting to overcome misfortune in their own life may draw inspiration from him since he is a testimony to the strength of resiliency and endurance.

Giving Back: Sylvester Stallone's Charity Donations and Philanthropic Activities

Aside from Stalones's flourishing career in Hollywood, Sylvester Stallone has dedicated much of his life to humanitarian work and philanthropic endeavors. He has contributed millions of dollars to several charities and organizations throughout the years, and he has made use of his platform to raise awareness of significant concerns. Supporting soldiers and military families has been one of Stallone's main charitable endeavors. He has spent several years working with the USO, a charity that assists military men and their families. Stallone has taken part in several USO tours, going to see the soldiers abroad and entertaining and encouraging them. Also, he has made large financial contributions to the organization, aiding in the funding of initiatives that support soldiers and their families.

He has also worked with the Special Olympics, an international group that gives intellectually disabled persons year-round access to sports instruction and physical competition. He has acted as an advocate for the group, assisting in the awareness- and money-raising efforts for its projects. To help the group's efforts to provide disabled people the chance to engage in sports and other activities, he has also contributed money to it. Stallone has been active with several other philanthropic groups in addition to his work with veterans and people with disabilities. He has contributed to organizations that encourage health and well-being, such as the Muscular Dystrophy Association and the Children's Miracle Network, as well as charities that provide resources and education to children from disadvantaged backgrounds.

Stallone's charity activities go beyond financial contributions and support for nonprofit organizations. He has also promoted significant problems using his famous status as a platform. He was chosen in 2005 to serve as a goodwill ambassador for the UN, with an emphasis on encouraging physical fitness and a healthy lifestyle. Also, he has promoted causes like animal welfare and environmental protection on social media. Ultimately, Stallone's humanitarian donations and philanthropic activities show his dedication to helping others and changing the world for the better. He continues to encourage people to support issues that are important to them by using his success and position to do so. Stallone has significantly improved the lives of numerous people via his work with veterans, persons with disabilities, and other humanitarian groups. He has also left a long-lasting legacy of compassion and goodwill. Stallone's commitment to charity and community service is a result of his principles and life experiences. He often leaned on people for assistance as a young, struggling actor to get by. He developed a strong feeling of appreciation as a result of this encounter, and throughout his professional life, he has prioritized helping people in need. Together with his charity donations, Stallone has taken part in several programs designed to mentor and inspire young people. He has given speeches at colleges and institutions, inspiring people to strive for their aspirations and never give up. Moreover, he has backed initiatives like the Young Storytellers Foundation that help young performers and filmmakers by offering guidance and tools.

Throughout the years, Stallone has received various honors and distinctions for his charitable work. The Academy of Motion Picture Arts and Sciences presented him with the Jean Hersholt

Humanitarian Award in 2016 in honor of his charitable endeavors. The honor is granted to those who have significantly aided humanitarian endeavors. Stallone maintains his modesty and commitment to utilizing his position to change the world despite his fame and money. He emphasizes the value of helping others and leveraging prosperity to do good deeds often. We must look out for one another since "we are all in this together," he has remarked. Ultimately, Stallone's charity work and services serve as an example for others. He has made a difference in the world and supported causes that are important to him by using his achievements and platform. His commitment to helping people and improving their lives is a monument to his character and serves as a reminder of the value of generosity, kindness, and goodness of heart.

The Stallone Legacy: How His Work Is Still an Inspiration to Future Generations of Filmmakers.

Sylvester Stallone has had a legendary career as an actor, screenwriter, and director. He has produced franchises that have lasted for several generations and portrayed some of the most iconic roles in movie history. His legacy continues to be an inspiration for the next generations of performers, fans, and filmmakers.

Stallone was raised in a working-class household and was born in New York City in 1946. Due to untreated dyslexia, he had trouble in school but found comfort in bodybuilding and athletics. Stallone started his acting career with modest parts in movies like "The Lords of Flatbush" and "Death Race 2000" after migrating to Hollywood in the 1970s. But what made him famous was his ground-breaking performance as the lead in "Rocky" in 1976.

The Rocky Road

The movie "Rocky" is about a struggling boxer who is allowed to compete for the heavyweight world title. Three Academy Awards, including Best Picture, were given to the movie, which was a critical and financial triumph. Stallone received an Academy Award nomination for Best Actor for his portrayal of Rocky Balboa, and he went on to feature in five other installments of the series.

Because of "Rocky," Stallone was able to explore other endeavors like the "Rambo" series. In the first movie, "First Blood," a Vietnam veteran was pushed too far by law enforcement in a small community. It was initially released in 1982. Three sequels to the box office success were produced. During the 1980s and 1990s, Stallone also appeared in several other popular movies, such as "Cobra," "Tango & Cash," and "Cliffhanger."

Stallone soon began writing and directing his movies as a result of his acting career. He co-wrote and performed in the 1978 drama

The Rocky Road

"Paradise Alley," about three brothers who want to leave their working-class backgrounds behind and become wrestlers. He continued to create and direct several additional movies, such as "Staying Alive," the Saturday Night Fever sequel, and the action-packed "The Expendables" trilogy.

New generations of filmmakers are constantly being inspired by Stallone's body of work. He has become a real legend of film because of his dedication to developing engaging characters and crafting engaging tales. As a result of his depiction of Rocky Balboa, he was also honored for his services to the cinema business by being inducted into the Boxing Hall of Fame.

Stallone's influence on culture goes beyond only the film industry. His recognizable figures and catchphrases are used in everything from commercials to video games, making him a cultural phenomenon. Several filmmakers and performers who have come after him have been influenced by his work.

The Rocky Road

Ryan Coogler, the "Creed" filmmaker, is one illustration of Stallone's ongoing effect on the movie business. The "Rocky" series served as inspiration for Coogler, who wanted to make a movie that both paid tribute to the original and told a fresh tale. The outcome was the highly praised movie "Creed," which follows Apollo Creed's kid as he prepares to be a boxer with the aid of Rocky Balboa. Stallone received a nomination for Best Supporting Actor at the Academy Awards as a result of the movie's box office and critical success.

Beyond the roles he has performed and the movies he has directed, Stallone has affected the film business. Also, he has promoted indie cinema and utilized his notoriety to help promote smaller, less well-known movies. Stallone established Balboa Productions in 1995 intending to make movies that otherwise may not have been created. Several movies have been made by the firm, including the highly regarded drama "Fruitvale Station," which was directed

The Rocky Road

by Ryan Coogler and recounts the last day of Oscar Grant's life after he was shot and murdered by a police officer in Oakland, California. Stallone has also promoted veterans' issues and utilized his influence to raise awareness of the difficulties that former service members experience. He established the Stallone Soldiers Foundation in 1985 to help soldiers and their families. The foundation has raised millions of dollars for charities that aid soldiers and has contributed to the provision of services for veterans who are battling PTSD and other problems.

Stallone's hardships and his capacity for overcoming adversity have also influenced his reputation. During his career, he has seen a lot of disappointments, such as countless box office and critical flops. He has, however, always been able to recover and go on developing gripping characters and narratives that connect with readers.

Stallone has become a role model for young actors and directors due to his commitment to his art and willingness to take chances. He has shown that success in the film business requires more than just skill; it also requires tenacity, hard effort, and a willingness to take risks. Stallone hasn't slowed down in recent years as he's been working on fresh projects. He reprised his role as Rocky Balboa in the "Creed" series, and he also had cameos in "Rambo: Last Blood" and "Guardians of the Galaxy Vol. 2."

Finally, Sylvester Stallone's impact continues to influence the next generations of performers and filmmakers. He has become a real legend of film because of his dedication to developing engaging characters and crafting engaging tales. His influence on pop culture is evident, and his commitment to independent cinema and veterans' issues has elevated him to the status of a role model for aspiring actors and performers. The success of Sylvester Stallone is proof of the value of patience, hard effort, and the capacity to rise above adversity.

Chapter 4

From Scripts to Screen: Stallone's Experience as a Screenwriter.

Sylvester Stallone is a skilled screenwriter. His breakout performance as Rocky Balboa in the 1976 movie "Rocky," which he also penned, marked the beginning of his career as a screenwriter. The movie was a critical and financial success; it won three Academy Awards, including Best Picture, and it helped start Sylvester Stallone's career as a significant figure in Hollywood.

He continued to write screenplays for both his movies and those of other directors after "Rocky" became a blockbuster. His most well-known roles throughout the years include John Rambo in the "Rambo" trilogy and Barney Ross in the "Expendables" series. He has authored the screenplays for several of these roles.

The Rocky Road

Stallone's aptitude for developing engrossing characters that are both larger-than-life and approachable is one of his skills as a screenwriter. His characters often experience intense internal strife and battle with inner demons, which adds to their complexity and intrigue. Also, he has a talent for crafting memorable and powerful language, which has contributed to the legendary status of many of his films.

Stallone's attention to detail is another quality of his scripting that has aided in his success. He devotes a lot of time to studying his themes and being fully immersed in the lives of his characters, which enables him to develop realistic and compelling tales and characters. This focus on detail can be seen in movies like "Rocky," which shows the world of professional boxing with accuracy, and "Rambo," which examines the terrible realities of war and how they affect troops.

The Rocky Road

Stallone's background as a screenwriter has also given him a unique insight into the filming process. He appreciates the value of teamwork and has often worked extensively with producers and directors to bring his screenplays to life. Among his most popular movies as a consequence of this partnership include "First Blood," which was directed by Ted Kotcheff, and "Rocky," which was helmed by John G. Avildsen.

Stallone has continued to write and create new ventures in recent years. In addition to having written the screenplay for the next movie "Samaritan," in which he also stars, he has also made plans to create a prequel to the "Rocky" series that would concentrate on the character's early years.

In conclusion, Sylvester Stallone's background as a screenwriter has contributed significantly to his career as a director. His attention to detail has produced storylines and characters that are real and convincing, and his ability to develop intriguing characters and write memorable language has contributed to the legendary status of many of his films. Stallone's background as a screenwriter has also given him a distinctive viewpoint on the movie-making process, which has aided him in working well with producers and directors. Ultimately, Stallone's success as one of Hollywood's most lasting and adored performers has been greatly influenced by his work as a screenwriter.

Behind the Scenes of the Famous Franchise: The Making of Rambo

One of the most recognizable and adored action film series of all time, the Rambo franchise has influenced culture for more than 40 years. Sylvester Stallone's portrayal of John Rambo has made him a cultural hero, and action movies have come to be associated with his catchphrases and characteristic headband. So what went into creating this illustrious franchise? We'll go deeper into the production process of the movie Rambo in this book.

The first installment of the Rambo series, "First Blood," was released in 1982 and was based on David Morrell's book of the same name. The story follows Vietnam War veteran John Rambo, who is driven to the edge by the acts of a small-town police department. "First Blood" became Sylvester Stallone's breakout action film and was a critical and financial triumph.

Because of "First Blood's" popularity, a follow-up film called "Rambo: First Blood Part II" was made in 1985. Rambo was sent back to Vietnam in this movie on a covert mission to free US prisoners of war. With over $300 million in global box office receipts, the movie was a resounding box office hit.

The third movie in the series, "Rambo III," was released in 1988. In this film, Rambo joined forces with the Afghan Mujahideen to battle the Soviet Union. Although "Rambo III" was likewise a financial success, it did not have the same level of popularity with spectators as the previous two movies and garnered negative reviews from critics.

With the 2008 release of "Rambo," the series was revitalized after a protracted absence. Rambo's journey to Burma in this film was to rescue a group of Christian missionaries who had been abducted by a ruthless military government. With nearly $113 million in global box office receipts, the film was a financial hit.

"Rambo: Last Blood," the most current film in the series, was published in 2019. As his niece is taken hostage by a Mexican drug gang in this film, Rambo embarks on a quest for vengeance. Despite the film's unfavorable critical reception, it was a box office hit, earning over $91 million globally.

The Rocky Road

What went into creating these enduring films, then? Let's look more closely.

It's crucial to remember that Sylvester Stallone's Rambo trilogy was a passion project from the beginning. Stallone not only played the lead role in each of the five films, but he also authored or co-wrote each one. He had a significant role in the franchise's development, and he gave each film his all-out effort.

The production of "First Blood" was difficult. Ted Kotcheff was initially slated to helm the film, but after clashing with Stallone, he was let go. George P. Cosmatos, Ted Kotcheff's successor, ended up directing the film. Stallone and the film's producers reportedly had disagreements about the conclusion, which Stallone thought was too depressing. He struggled to have a happier conclusion, and he ultimately succeeded.

The production of "Rambo: First Blood Part 2" was extremely difficult. Russell Mulcahy was initially slated to helm the film, but following disputes with Stallone, he was let go. George P. Cosmatos, who had previously collaborated with Stallone on the film "Cobra," ended up directing the film. Also, Stallone and the film's producers had a political disagreement. The film received criticism for its jingoistic tone and how it depicted Vietnam.

Stallone as Director: Exploring His Work Behind the Camera.

Sylvester Stallone has established himself as a successful filmmaker. He has made several movies throughout the years that have shown his abilities as a director. Let's examine a few of Stallone's films from the director's perspective.
The sequel to the well-liked movie "Saturday Night Fever," "Staying Alive," was released in 1983, and Sylvester Stallone took on the difficult task of directing it. While there were some negative reviews, the movie was a box office hit and proved Stallone had filmmaking talent. The second installment in the "Rocky" series,

The Rocky Road

"Rocky II," was directed by Stallone and starts up where the previous movie left off. Stallone's reputation as a triple threat—a writer, director, and actor—was cemented by the movie's critical and economic success. Stallone continues to direct the "Rocky" series with this third entry, "Rocky III," released in 1982. Another box office success, the movie featured Mr. T as the antagonist. Strong performances from Stallone's actors were aided by his directing, which also gave the battle sequences more life.

"Rambo" (2008) - Stallone once again played the role of John Rambo in this fourth installment of the series. The movie was a commercial success and received plaudits for its action scenes. The movie was noted for having a gritty, realistic atmosphere because of Stallone's directing.

"The Expendables" (2010) was an action-packed film that Stallone both directed and acted in, bringing together some of the greatest stars in the action genre. The movie, which was a love

63

letter to the action flicks of the 1980s and 1990s, was a financial hit.

"Rocky Balboa" (2006) - Stallone made his acting and directing comebacks to the "Rocky" series with this film. Both reviewers and viewers praised it for its emotional resonance and Sylvester Stallone's nuanced performance, and it was highly received by both groups.

"Paradise Alley" (1978) - This was Stallone's directorial debut, and the movie is about three brothers who want to become wrestlers to leave their undesirable neighborhood. The movie received plaudits for its realism and outstanding performances even if it wasn't a major commercial hit.

Although Stallone didn't direct "The Lords of Flatbush" (1974), which was co-directed by Martin Davidson and Stephen Verona, he did contribute to the story and play one of the key parts. The film, which is about a gang of Brooklyn teens in the 1950s, received plaudits

The Rocky Road

for its accurate depiction of adolescent life. Stallone has shown a knack for acting, writing, and directing throughout his career. His movies often deal with themes like tenacity, the victory of the underdog, and the resilience of the human spirit. Although some of his films have drawn flak for being predictable, others have won praise for their rich emotional content and endearing characters.

Stallone's flexibility as an artist has also been shown through his work as a filmmaker. While he is most renowned for his action movies, he has also directed comedies and tragedies. He has consistently been prepared to take chances and attempt new things, regardless of the genre, which is why he has been a mainstay in Hollywood for more than 40 years.

Stallone's working relationships with other actors and filmmakers (Collaborators with Co-Stars)

Over the years, Sylvester Stallone has collaborated with a broad variety of actors and directors, developing close professional bonds with several of them. Below are some of his most illustrious partners and co-stars.

- Carl Weathers - In the "Rocky" movies, Weathers portrayed Apollo Creed, a character who had a complicated connection with Sylvester Stallone's Rocky Balboa. During numerous movies, Weathers and Stallone had a close professional connection, and Weathers has said that Stallone was essential in his growth as an actor.
- Dolph Lundgren-commanding Lundgren's physical presence in "Rocky IVfinal "'s fight sequence made it one of the franchise's most memorable. Lundgren portrayed the intimidating Russian boxer,

The Rocky Road

Ivan Drago. Throughout the years, Stallone and Lundgren have remained friends and collaborated on several other projects, including "The Expendables" film series.

- Stallone and Arnold Schwarzenegger, two of the most recognizable action performers of all time, have collaborated on several movies, including "Escape Plan" and "The Expendables." Despite their on-screen competition, the two actors get along well off-screen and often complement one another's performances. The first "Rocky" movie was directed by John G. Avildsen, who worked with Sylvester Stallone to produce one of the most adored movies of all time. Stallone has said that Avildsen helped him improve as a director. The two stayed close until Avildsen passed away in 2017.
- Michael B. Jordan played Adonis Creed, the son of Apollo Creed, in the "Rocky" spinoff movie "Creed". Stallone co-wrote the screenplay with Jordan and had a

supporting part in the movie. Together, they were able to update the "Rocky" series while still paying homage to the first movies in the series and adding something new and exciting.

During his career, Stallone has collaborated with a broad variety of outstanding actors and directors and developed close working ties with several of them. Some of the most iconic and cherished movies in Hollywood history have been made possible by these partnerships.

Chapter 5

Stallone's Reflections on his life and Career: Moral Lessons Learned

Sylvester Stallone has gone through spectacular highs and heartbreaking lows during his career, but he has never wavered in his dedication to his profession or his love for the movies he makes.

The Rocky Road

These are some of Stallone's observations on his career and the lessons he has discovered thus far:

A.)Perseverance is Essential: Stallone has often discussed how he overcame various challenges to succeed as an actor and director. When he was told he lacked the ability or attractive looks, he still clung to his ideals. According to Stallone, his capacity to persevere in the face of difficulty and never give up has been the secret to his success. Stallone is renowned for taking chances in his movies, whether it's pushing the limits of the action genre or examining challenging emotional topics. According to him, being creative is being ready to attempt new things and taking chances, even if they don't turn out to be successful. Stallone has had tremendous professional success, but he is keen to tell people that it hasn't always been simple. Achievement is a journey, not a destination. According to him, the key to maintaining motivation is to concentrate on the act of producing something fresh and worthwhile. Success, he contends, is a process rather than a destination.

B.)The partnership is Crucial: Stallone has collaborated with many excellent writers, directors, and performers over the years, and he thinks that great art is only possible with strong teamwork. He's always been receptive to suggestions and criticism from his colleagues, and he feels that sharing the creative process with others has aided in his development as an artist.

C.)Never Stop Learning: Stallone is always seeking new difficulties and chances to develop. He doesn't hesitate to take on challenging jobs or attempt new things.

D.)Self-Belief and Confidence: Even when others questioned him, Stallone had confidence in himself and his skills. Despite being an unknown actor at the time, he insisted on writing the screenplay for "Rocky" and taking the starring role. He finally saw success at the box office and critical praise as a result of his self-belief and faith in his skills.

E.)Accept Your Flaws and Imperfections: "Rocky" struck a chord with viewers all around the globe because he had flaws and imperfections, just like any other regular person. Stallone's ability to depict a realistic character taught us that faults and defects are OK; what counts is how we handle difficulties and work to become better people.

F.)Never Compromise Your Integrity: Stallone maintained his creative integrity throughout his career and was committed to his ideas for the roles he played. Even though he was offered substantial amounts of money, he refused to sell the rights to "Rocky" unless he was permitted to appear in the movie. This reminds us how crucial it is to stick to our morals and ideals.

G.)Humility and Gratitude: Stallone maintained his humility and gratitude for his accomplishments while reaching the height of prosperity. He saw how others had helped him succeed and how chance and luck had played a part in his path.

H.)Accept Second Chances: Sylvester Stallone's career revival in the 2000s with the "Rocky" and "Rambo" franchises showed the value of second chances. He demonstrated to us that failures are not the end, but rather a springboard for even bigger successes.

In conclusion, Sylvester Stallone's life story is full of inspirational and motivating moral lessons that may help us to follow our goals, have faith in ourselves, and never give up, even in the face of hardship. His life serves as a motivating example of how hard effort, persistence, self-belief, and a commitment to one's principles may lead to greatness.

Stallone's Accolades and Recognition for his Work.

The Rocky Road

At the Oscars and other awards ceremonies. Hollywood has benefited much from Sylvester Stallone's career, and his contributions have received several honors and awards throughout the years. The Rocky Balboa character in the "Rocky" film series, which has played a significant part in his career, is maybe his most well-known role. For his role in the first "Rocky" movie, Sylvester Stallone received an Academy Award nomination for Best Actor. He later received another nomination in the same category for the movie "Creed." With "Rocky," he was nominated for Best Original Screenplay as well. Stallone has received several honors for his role in the "Rocky" series, including the Screen Actors Guild Award for Outstanding Performance by a Male Actor in a Supporting Role and the Golden Globe Award for Best Supporting Actor for "Creed."

Stallone has received praise for his efforts in other movies outside the "Rocky" series. For his performance in "First Blood," he received a

Golden Globe nomination for Best Actor. He also received a People's Choice Award for Favorite Action Movie Star for his work in the "Rambo" series.

Moreover, Stallone has received honorary accolades including the Hollywood Film Festival's Career Achievement Award and the Golden Globe Award for Lifetime Achievement in Motion Pictures.

In general, Sylvester Stallone has had a prosperous career in Hollywood, and his contributions have received several honors and prizes.

Printed in Great Britain
by Amazon